LINCOLNWOOD PUBLIC LIBRARY
W9-CEC-470

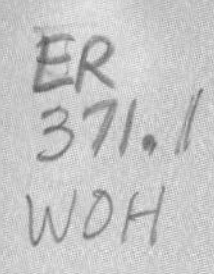

Community Workers

Helping You Learn

A Book About Teachers

Sarah C. Wohlrabe
Illustrated by Eric Thomas

Thanks to our advisers for their expertise, research, knowledge, and advice:

Duane Udstuen, Ed.S., Adjunct Professor and Associate Director,
Master of Arts in Education Program, Saint Mary's University of Minnesota, Minneapolis, Minnesota

Susan Kesselring, M.A., Literacy Educator
Rosemount-Apple Valley-Eagan (Minnesota) School District

PICTURE WINDOW BOOKS
Minneapolis, Minnesota

To my favorite educator of them all. Thanks, Dad! —S.C.W.

Managing Editor: Bob Temple
Creative Director: Terri Foley
Editor: Peggy Henrikson
Editorial Adviser: Andrea Cascardi
Copy Editor: Laurie Kahn
Designer: John Moldstad
Page production: Picture Window Books
The illustrations in this book were prepared digitally.

Picture Window Books
5115 Excelsior Boulevard
Suite 232
Minneapolis, MN 55416
1-877-845-8392
www.picturewindowbooks.com

Printed in the United States of America.

Library of Congress Cataloging-in-Publication Data
Wohlrabe, Sarah C., 1976–
Helping you learn : a book about teachers / written by
Sarah C. Wohlrabe ; illustrated by Eric Thomas.
p. cm. — (Community workers)
Summary: Describes some of the things that teachers do to help people learn.
Includes bibliographical references and index.
ISBN 1-4048-0084-0
1. Teachers—Juvenile literature. [1. Teachers. 2. Occupations.] I. Thomas, Eric, ill. II. Title.
III. Community workers (Picture Window Books)
LB1775 .W54 2004
371.2—dc21

2003004197

The world is full
of exciting things
to learn.

Where do you start?
Teachers can help you.

Teachers always greet you with a smile.

Hello and welcome,
boys and girls.

Teachers help you
write a little a
and a big A

and sound out
big words.

Teachers show you how to measure
from your heel to your toes,

read the clock,

and count up high.

A teacher can be the coach

or the referee.

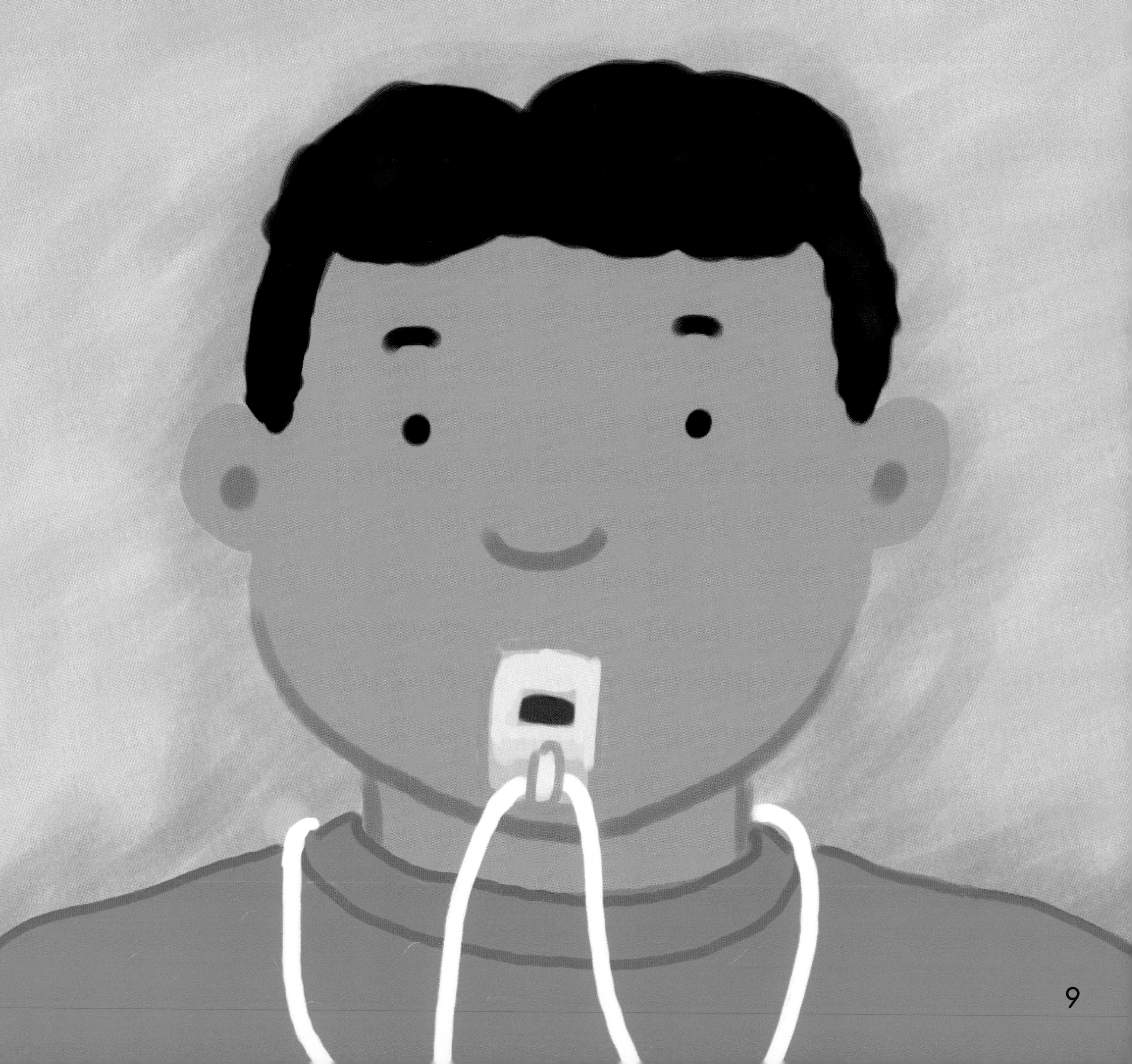

Teachers take you places on a school bus

and in your imagination.

Teachers give you courage to do your best.

and in your imagination.

Once upon
a time …

Teachers give you courage to do your best.

They tell your parents about the great work you've done.

Teachers let you help with important jobs.

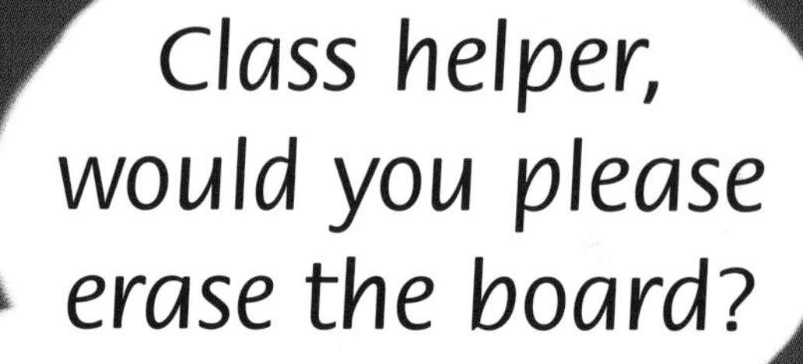

They might even let you
take care of little critters.

Teachers help you send
an e-mail around the world

and learn about the country it reaches.

Teachers care about you.

They want you to grow in lots of ways.

Teachers help you learn.

Did You Know?

- There were teachers even before books were invented. Teachers had to memorize all their lessons and pass them on by repeating them to their students.
- Worldwide, more people work in teaching than in any other job.
- Long ago, only boys went to school. Girls were taught at home by their mothers.
- Going to school in the United States became the law in every state by 1918.
- Some people live too far from any town to go to school. In some places, these people listen to teachers on the radio. In other places, people with computers take classes over the Internet. Radio and Internet teachers usually never see their students.
- Students learn in different ways. Some students learn best by listening. Others learn best by reading. Many learn best with hands-on activities. Teachers have to find creative ways to help all kinds of learners.
- Teachers are students, too. They read articles and go to meetings to learn new ideas about teaching. Many teachers spend their summer vacations taking college classes.

Teacher Idea Web

An idea web is a good way to help you sort information. Use the idea web that's started below to make your own idea web about teachers. Copy this web onto your own sheet of paper. Use the ideas in this book to make the web bigger. Then add your own ideas.

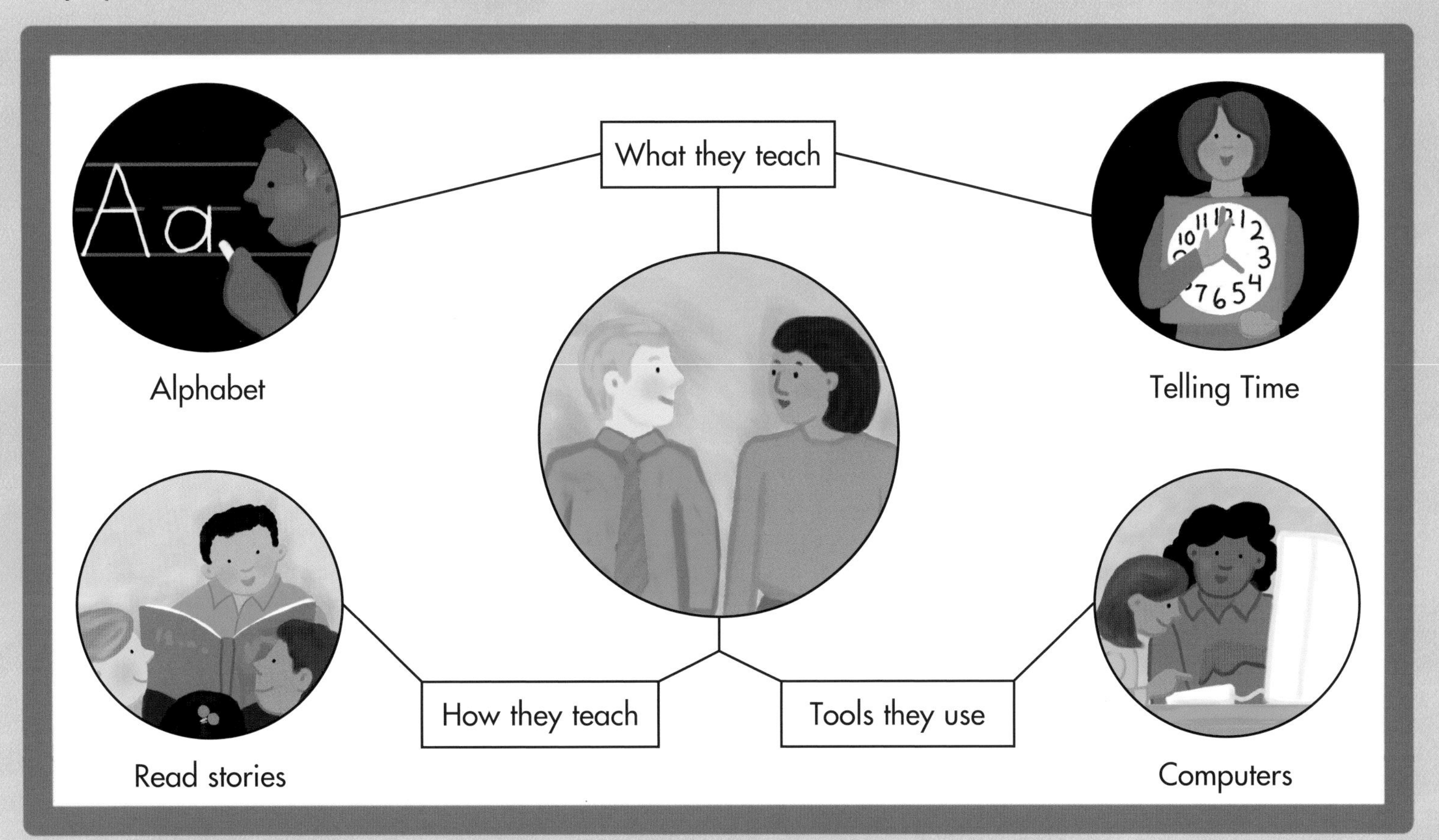

Words to Know

coach (KOHCH) – someone who trains a sports team

courage (KUR-ij) – bravery

e-mail (EE-mayl) – messages sent by computer over phone lines. The "e" in e-mail stands for electronic.

imagination (i-maj-uh-NAY-shuhn) – the ability to make things up in your mind or think of things you can't actually see

Internet (IN-tur-net) – a system that connects computers all over the world. The Internet is used to send e-mail.

memorize (MEM-uh-rize) – to learn something by heart so you can remember it without looking it up

referee (ref-uh-REE) – someone who makes sure that all the players in a game are following the rules. A referee makes sure everything is fair.

To Learn More

At the Library

Allard, Harry. *Miss Nelson Is Missing!* Boston: Houghton Mifflin, 1977.
Flanagan, Alice K. *Teachers.* Minneapolis: Compass Point Books, 2001.
Lehn, Barbara. *What Is a Teacher?* Brookfield, Conn.: Millbrook Press, 2000.
Wood, Douglas. *What Teachers Can't Do.* New York: Simon & Schuster, 2002.

On the Web

Bureau of Labor Statistics (BLS) Career Information: Teachers
For information about what K-12 teachers do,
what the job is like, how to prepare for it, and more
http://stats.bls.gov/k12/html/red_002.htm

Fact Hound
Want more information about teachers?
Fact Hound offers a safe, fun way to find Web sites related to this book.
All of the sites on Fact Hound have been researched by our staff.
http://www.facthound.com

1. Visit the Fact Hound home page.
2. Enter a search word related to this book, or type in this special code: 1404800840.
3. Click on the FETCH IT button.

Your trusty Fact Hound will fetch the best sites for you!

Index

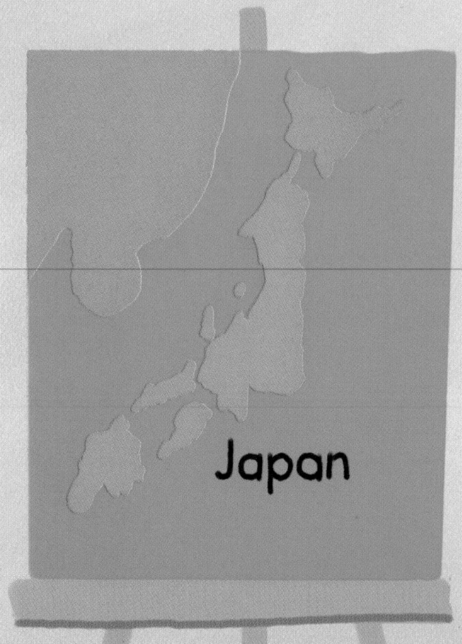